*If all flowers wanted to be roses, Nature would lose her springtime beauty, and the fields would no longer be decked out with little wildflowers.*

Saint Therese of Lisieux

Edle Catharina Norman

# Beautiful Wildflowers

## wedding bouquets, arrangements & more from nature's seasonal abundance

SELLERS
PUBLISHING

## Note to Readers

The wildflowers mentioned in this book may vary in availability,
depending on the region of the country where you live. If you
cannot locate a certain wildflower in your area, please feel free
to make appropriate substitutions.

First published in 2005 as
*Vakre Markblomster*
by Edle Catharina Norman
copyright 2005 © Cappelen Damm AS

## Published by Sellers Publishing, Inc.

English translation copyright © 2014 Sellers Publishing, Inc.
All rights reserved.

Edited by Robin Haywood.
Translated from Norwegian by Margaret Berge Hartge.
Production layout by Charlotte Cromwell

Sellers Publishing, Inc.
161 John Roberts Road, South Portland, Maine 04106
Visit our Web site: www.sellerspublishing.com
E-mail: rsp@rsvp.com

ISBN 13: 978-1-4162-4503-2
Library of Congress Control Number: 2013945238

10 9 8 7 6 5 4 3 2 1

Printed and bound in China.

Also by Edle Catharina Norman
*Beautiful Winter* (ISBN 13: 978-1-4162-0847-1)

# Contents

# Introduction
## *Welcome to My Fairy-Tale World*

I have always loved nature and how every season brings something new. In spring and summer, I pick bouquets of hepatica (a small woodland treasure that blooms in very early spring and reaches 3–6 inches tall), wood anemone, and other wild plants. Upon arriving home, I place them in vases and feel uplifted as I admire their beauty and their wildness.

When my children's great-grandmother, Olle, died some years ago, my brother-in-law suggested that instead of ordering a wreath made from cultivated flowers, we could create our own. He put together a beautifully simple one using spruce twigs he found in the forest. I decided to decorate it a little bit, and I went into the woods and chose some unripe cloudberries (raspberries will also work), grass of Parnassus (*Parnassia* palustris, a stunning white marsh wildflower found in Alaska, Oregon, and across the Great Lakes region into upstate New York), bluebells, juniper twigs, lichen, and heather. I worked outside the entire afternoon, placing the brightly colored flowers in between the spruce twigs and thinking about Olle and life in general. Deep in reflection, I experienced strong feelings of my own well-being and a sense of harmony with the world around me.

I was surprised that the many friends who saw the decorated wreath loved it. A while later, I made another wreath with what I found outside my cabin door near Oslo,

*The author with a late summer wildflower harvest of bluebells, yarrow, wild poppies, daisies, rose hips, and many other colorful flowers.*

and those who saw it reacted with the same enthusiasm they had shown before. Consequently, whenever I went hiking in the forest, I trained myself to really see all that was before me, to discover the beauty of a bud about to open or of wildflowers golden in the sunlight, and to gather all the natural materials I could possibly use. All the while, as I walked around and collected the bounty of rich fields and ditches, I felt a powerful sense of joy. Even in the city, I came across areas where bluebells, primroses, or sun spurge (*Euphorbia*) grew here and there; it made me so happy that you would have thought that I had stumbled upon a secret treasure! Once home, I sat down in the peace and quiet, and my hands would go to work, grouping and pinning and arranging what I had found. Again, the response was so positive to my creations that it increased the delight I felt in my work. Then an idea struck — yes, to borrow an old cliche — just like a bolt of lightning from the sky: I wanted to spend the rest of my life doing this!

So, I have been doing just that, and it has been like a fairy-tale journey constantly filled with new discoveries — because from the least noticeable plant, the smallest crowns of seeds or hulls, and what others would call weeds, something beautiful can be created. My love of nature has not diminished at all.

During these years, I developed my own techniques. Additionally, my knowledge about wildflowers and wild plants has grown considerably. Since any bridal bouquet or wreath I created had to last at least a couple of days, I learned about the fields where I could find the best flowers and what bloomed when. Which flowers will keep for a long time without water, and which must be continuously in water? This is the knowledge I wish to share with readers:

1. Gathering and treatment of flowers and natural materials

2. Tools and equipment

3. Techniques for binding stems and twigs

4. Aesthetics

We are touched by the beauty of wreaths, decorations, and bouquets made from wild plants; they make such an impression. Cultivated flowers are available throughout the year, and I occasionally use them in my work when a special touch of color or texture is needed — you'll see my use of orchids, especially (because I love them!), in the book.

It used to be that cultivated flowers were the ones we bought for special occasions, while wildflowers that could be picked out the back door were for every day. It is now the opposite. In our busy lives, we quickly grab a ready-made bouquet when time is short; wildflowers have become exclusive. While cultivated flowers exist almost everywhere, wildflowers are not always available. Suddenly, during spring, there they are, and the sight moves us. Wildflowers speak to our emotional life. They remind us of happy times during childhood — those moments when we felt a spontaneous burst of joy upon finding the first buttercups of summer, and our mother's smiling face when we gave her the bouquet we had picked. Just to hold flowers or moss or reindeer lichen brings back good memories and fills me with a sense of peace and of being one with nature. So, dear readers, I hope that you will seek out all that nature has to offer and feel inspiration flow within you as you create beautiful bouquets and arrangements that will lift your spirits in any season.

Edle Catharina Norman
Oslo, Norway

# Gathering & Treatment
## of flowers and natural materials

As you go on your favorite walks in the woods, look around. You'll see a wide array of flowers, greenery, lichen, and berries growing in ditches, boggy areas, and meadows. Some are present in spring and summer, while others show up during fall. Allow yourself to be lured out into nature's own treasure chest, and gather a most luxuriant and colorful bounty!

*A weekend of gathering will guarantee enough flowers for many decorations in the coming weeks: dooryard dock (Rumex longifolius; plentiful in almost all of North America), Jacob's ladder (Polemonium vanbruntiae; common in the northeastern U.S.) tansy, yarrow, yellow chamomile, poppies, daisies, bluebells, and wild celery (Vallisneria americana; found mainly in eastern North America). In the background you can see juniper and dwarf birch branches.*

When you are out gathering flowers and natural materials for your projects, here are a few tips to keep in mind to make the process as fun and effective as possible, and to help your plants last longer, too:

• If possible, bring a bucket containing some water and place the materials in it right after cutting. Sometimes it just won't work to carry a vessel into the forest, but there is another option. Place moist paper towels (the strong ones that won't disintegrate) in individual plastic bags. After you've cut the stems, put a rubber band around the bottom to gather them, wrap them with the paper towels, place them in the bag, and secure it with a twisty tie.

• Pick one bunch of a particular type of flower at a time, and endeavor to get as much of the stem as you can manage, since the longer the stem, the more options you have in arranging. Gather the ends of the stems, wrap a rubber band around them, trim them on the diagonal with a sharp knife, and place them immediately in water. By cutting the stems when the flowers are bunched, you will get stems of various lengths, which can come in handy.

Certain types of flowers, such as wood anemones, lily of the valley, and grass of Parnassus, should not be pinched off, but pulled straight up. By doing this, you will get the longest stems possible. When you are picking flowers with tough stems, use a small flower knife and "pick" with the knife. This will keep you from pulling up the roots.

*Wood anemones (Anemone quinquefolia), woodland plants with deeply divided leaves and a single, showy, white-to-pinkish flower.*

Many people complain that wildflowers last for such a short time. Learn to discern between older and younger plants, and pick primarily the newly opened flowers. Lily of the valley, for example, should have several buds at the top of the stem. The yellow center of a daisy should be flat, without any arching. The same goes for the tansy. The bluebells' stigma should not be divided. The wood anemone's fruit bud should be light green and woolly, not dark green and smooth.

• After you've gathered the flowers and returned home, you'll begin the most important preparations: the leaves must be removed from the stems so that they do not come into contact with the water and create bacteria growth. The bacteria, if allowed to develop, will greatly reduce

*A meadow at midsummer with wildflowers, including bluebells yarrow, and Queen Anne's lace.*

the longevity of the flowers. Rinse every single stem, and keep only the upper leaves. Even the few leaves on the bluebells must go. Gather the flower stems and cut them on the diagonal before placing in water.

- The colder the temperature at which you store the flowers, the longer they will last.

- Lichen, corky fungi, moss, chestnuts, conifer cones, etc., must be dried before storing or they will rot. Place them on newspapers to dry. These natural materials can also be treated by placing them in the oven at 200–285°F (100–140° C) from five minutes to one hour to get rid of all the insects.

- We must, of course, not pick protected flowers. Different countries have different plants on their "protected species" lists, so make certain you are familiar with the flowers that are on the list where you live.

*Above is a yellow globe flower, not easily found in North America, but there are good substitutions, including the desert globemallow (Sphaeralcea ambigua), found in the dry western regions of the U.S. and coreopsis or tickseed (Coreopsis lanceolata), which grows almost everywhere in the U.S. in late spring.*

# Tools & Equipment

Your hands are your most important tools when you are making flowers arrangements; they have "the last word." However, the tools mentioned below will help by making your work easier and the results even better than if you only used your hands.

## Knife

Your knife must always be sharp. Your cuts will then be straight as you cut the flower stems. Straight cuts are essential for maximizing the flower's water absorption and thereby its longevity. You may use less expensive knives that have blades which can be replaced as they get dull.

## Scissors & Shears

Small wire scissors (wire cutters) are indispensable. You will use this tool to make clean cuts in the floral wire. You can actually use them for almost anything.

An ordinary pair of scissors can be used to cut raffia, silk ribbons, strings, and similar things, in addition to birch bark.

Pinking shears are just the tool for finishing off your birch-bark pieces.

You can use gardening shears to cut thicker branches from birch trees, junipers, and other greeneries that have wooden stalks.

## Pliers

It is practical to use cutting pliers for the heavier metal wires. You can also use them to twist one or more wires together.

## Die cutters & gouges

Die cutters are available in many different sizes. You will use them primarily to cut birch bark. If you are going to make many place cards, a die cutter that makes circles with a 2⅜-inch diameter is indispensable. You can use the gouges to make smaller holes for sewing and "locking stick" holes for the birch-bark vases and other birch-bark items.

## Hammer

You can use a hammer when working with gouges.

## Drill

An electric drill is very useful for making holes in the place-card pedestals, corky fungi, and other similar materials.

## Floral wire

Cut metal wires of different lengths and gauges are used for fastening (also called "pinning") conifer cones, rose hips, flowers, and similar greenery. Floral wires are also used to make bouquet holders with birch branches and wires. We make our own staples by bending short metal wires and cutting both ends so that they are sharp. I prefer unvarnished metal wires.

## Spool wire

This wire is softer than floral wire and comes on a spool. It is used for making wreaths, forming metal constructions, tying branches together, and similar work. I prefer the unvarnished kind. Copper-, silver-, or gold-colored wires can be very decorative.

## Stem wire

This wire also comes on a spool. It is very thin and can be used to wrap, for example, myrtle or heather. We use it to tie thin branches and twigs together. It is available in many different colors, but I prefer brown.

## Floral tape

We use this elastic tape frequently to wrap around floral wires. The brown-colored tape is the most practical. Stretch the tape as you are wrapping and overlap the wrappings. The tape will stick together from the heat of your hands. Floral tape is used to make the flowers stay more solidly in place in a bouquet, and to avoid getting rust in the water by covering the wire holder.

## Other equipment

In addition to the tools listed previously, you may need a measuring tape, a stapler, a darning needle, a permanent marker, a spray bottle, rubber bands, string, rope, jute yarn, raffia, a glue gun, a glue pan, plastic sheets, and a pencil.

Most of the tools and equipment can be bought at hardware stores, floral shops, or craft stores.

# Useful Information

In order to achieve optimum results, here's some advice that will come in handy:

## Grouping & repetition

Almost regardless of what you are going to make, you should group the flowers, keeping the same types and colors bunched together. This will make the composition seem less busy. A grouping that appears to be spread out or disorganized can look messy. To achieve a sense of balance, repeat the same grouping several places in the decoration.

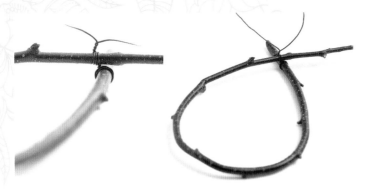

## Joining two branches

When you are going to attach one branch to another, whether in a circle or adding a new branch, first wrap spool wire two to three times around one branch, then lock the wrapping by twisting the wire ends a couple of times tightly around each other. Continue by wrapping the wire two to three times around the other branch and lock the wires by twisting them as before. Doing it this way will keep the branches in place, and it will look a lot nicer than if you wrapped both branches together at the same time! Don't cut the wires until all the work is done. You may want to attach another branch at the same place later.

## Softening branches

It's often necessary to soften branches — especially any thick ends — for easier shaping in twig decorations. See the accompanying photograph: Hold your hands around the branch, closely together, with one thumb beside the other. Bend the branch by moving the hands carefully away from each other without loosening your grip (you may want to wear gloves). Move your hands up along the entire branch, bending as you go. Start from the beginning again, and continue until the branch is pliable and soft. If you cheat on this process, you risk breaking the branch.

## Joining two floral wires

When making a metal construction, you must tie several wires together to get the desired length. Place two wires crossed over each other, about 2 inches from the ends, and twist each short end around each other. If you are going to attach a stem wire to a construction, wrap about 2 inches of the stem wire around the existing construction.

## Pinning

When you want to use flowers, rose hips, berries, or fungi with short stems, you must lengthen their stems by pinning them to a wire (see photograph

of pinned berries and seed pods on page 16). Bend the floral wire, place it alongside the plant's stem, and wrap one leg of the wire around the stem of the plant and around the other leg of the wire. Match the wire's thickness to the weight of what it will carry. You must wrap the wire stem with floral tape if you are using your pinned item in a bouquet. The floral tape will make the pinned stem stick to the other stems and not slide out. If your rose hip is lacking a stem, you can push the floral wire straight through the bottom of the rose hip and wrap the short end of the wire around the long end.

## Water containers

### Test tubes

These are made from transparent glass and can be bought in many different sizes. Attach them to the decoration with stem wire or spool wire. You can let the glass show in the decoration if you wish.

*Plastic test tubes with rubber tops*
These plastic flower tubes are not meant to be visible in the decoration.

*Pinned plastic test tube with rubber top.*

## Floral foam

*Wet floral foam* can only be used once. You can readily buy it in floral shops or hobby stores, and it comes in many shapes: balls, wreaths, bars, self-attaching mini sizes, and large sheets. Place the floral foam in water. When it sinks, after a few minutes, it is soaked through and ready to be used.

*Dry floral foam* is used in decorations with dry natural materials. You can either pin or glue it in place.

## Markers

Always use a permanent marker when you write on birch bark. You can also apply a marker to cover lighter cut surfaces on branches, if they are not an intended part of the design.

## Tips

The materials above are pinned with spool wire, but instead of using wire, you can fasten the materials to a straw wreath with greening pins. When doing this, you can use longer twigs.

You can decorate the wreath with lichen, pinecones, lichen, twigs, rose hips, berries, etc.

## Chlorine wash

All vases and glass containers should be rinsed in chlorine water to kill bacteria. The tape-covered handles of metal or birch bouquet holders should also be dipped in chlorine water before using.

## Leaves

Make sure that there are no leaves below the place you tie your bouquet together. Leaves in the water increase the growth of bacteria.

## Natural materials

If you do not have time to gather natural materials in the forests, meadows, or mountains, you can buy them at floral shops or hobby stores.

## Flowers

You can substitute cultivated flowers for wildflowers, and the other way around as well, in most of these decorations.

## Funerary decorations

In addition to the wreaths, most of the bouquets in this book can be used as appropriate decorations at a funeral or memorial service, especially if accompanied by a commemorative message written on birch bark. By making the arrangement yourself out of natural materials, you can create a display that is very special and personalized.

# Bouquets & Holders

*Wood anemones make a beautiful bouquet. They are at once delicate and sturdy, with a lovely yellow interior.*

*(opposite page)*
*A twig vase (see page 112) is a naturally decorative way to display wildflowers. This wildly colorful summer bouquet is composed of yellow and orange Siberian poppies (found most frequently in my country of Norway), combined with airy, light-green lady's mantle.*

# Flower Bouquets

*A bouquet of coltsfoot or bluebells (Mertensia), loosely arranged in a jar, creates the first real hint of spring when placed on the kitchen table. Later on, bouquets of wood anemones (Anemone quinquefolia) arrive, to be followed by early summer flowers in a multitude of colors: lily of the valley, marsh marigolds, red clover, and many others.*

A wildflower bouquet in a decorated vase adds a beautiful touch to any table and may even conjure up some happy childhood memories. You can easily create a stylish arrangement by placing lily of the valley flowers in an attractive birch-bark vase (see page 24) and mixing in some yellow-green lady's mantle. Bluebells or poppies, along with greens from the lingonberry bush *(Vaccinium vitis-idaea),* can also make colorful and delightful bouquets. The lingonberry is a small, evergreen shrub with edible red berries, similar to the cranberry. It typically grows in low, dense mats. Its young stems are green, and they work well in bouquets as they bring a distinctive texture with their fine, soft hairs; they become darker and hairless with age. Lingonberry bushes are found growing wild in almost all nothern states and in the Rocky Mountains.

A bouquet can, of course, be composed of many different types of flowers. A luxuriant gathering of all the flowers that bloom at midsummer, both large and small, may be charming, but it will probably not have the impact you want to use to decorate a table set for a party. You can come up with a much more striking bouquet by featuring just a few select types and colors of flowers. If you want to use all the midsummer flowers

at once, you'll achieve the best result by placing each type of flower in its own simple vase and then arranging the vases and colors harmoniously on the table.

## Binding the Flowers

The process of gathering the flower stems and rotating them in a circular motion is called "spiral binding." Begin by holding a bunch of green leaves in your hand. Place the flowers next to the greenery, initially arranging the stems vertically, straight and parallel to the leaves. As the bouquet grows, start putting the stems more at an angle, towards the right. Make sure all the stems are facing in the same direction. Turn the bouquet continuously in your hand. When the flowers are in a spiral, you can easily insert new flowers anywhere into the bouquet where there is a need for more. But — watch out — if the stems crisscross each other, it is almost impossible to insert any additional flowers.

## Fillers

To "lock" the flowers in a desired position, and to create space and depth in a bouquet, you can use fillers. Fillers are usually short, green leaves with long stems that are pinned with florist wire covered in floral tape. Place the fillers on the outside of the flower stalks, deeply in the bouquet. Twigs from blueberry bushes are very good to use, and they can bring height to the bouquet (see photograph below). Twigs from the lingonberry plant are also ideal.

# Birch-Bark Bouquet Holder & Vase

## Materials

* birch bark
* glass jars
* gouge or drill
* slow-drying glue
* stapler
* natural-colored string and a sewing needle to accommodate the size of the string
* juniper stick
* paper clips
* pencil
* needle
* paper
* cardboard
* pinking shears

*Birch-bark vases are unique and look lovely with both wildflowers and cultivated flowers. Add a touch of the natural world inside your home and use your vase over and over again.*

*The bark from fallen birch trees may be gathered at any time, but the best season for collecting live birch bark is spring. The bark is its thickest then, retaining the dark-brown inner bark which formed from flowing sap in winter. In spring, the bark will easily peel from the tree, and there's plenty of time for the tree to regrow the bark for the next winter — but don't take too much from any one tree, particularly a diseased or damaged one.*

*To store fresh bark for later use, lay out the sheets, back to back, and gently press them flat. Place light weights on top to prevent the bark from curling. Uncover, restack, and turn every couple of days. If stored bark or bark from fallen trees is used, the bark should be soaked in warm water for a day or even overnight; this will render even old bark pliable enough to be cut and bent. If the bark is very thick, several layers of the white bark may be peeled away to make the remaining sheet easier to cut or fold.*

## Instructions

This bouquet holder is perfect for a bride and the members of her wedding party, plus the size is easy to adjust for a flower girl.

* Use the pattern on page 136, it will fit a small jar with a diameter of approximately 1½ inches and 3¼ inches high. Photocopy it, cut it out, and place the left side under the right. Align the black dots and the sewing "lines."Lightly tape the sides together and see how the size will work for you. If you have small hands, roll it a bit tighter, making sure that you keep the "tepee" shape and enough room to put a jar inside for the bouquet.

24

* Once your size is determined, punch out the holes and the smaller dots for sewing lines on the pattern.

* If you think you'll make other bouquet holders, then transfer the pattern onto smooth, stiff cardboard, but move the bottom line $\frac{1}{16}$–$\frac{1}{8}$ inch downwards. You now have a pattern you can use repeatedly.

* Place the pattern on a piece of birch bark. Trace around the pattern and mark the holes. Cut it out and punch the holes (see photo number 1, at right). You can choose which side of the birch bark will be on the outside. Use sturdy pinking shears to make a zigzag cut on the overlapping flap.

* Prepare an adequately long and thin juniper stick or other pliable, sturdy twig, and stick it through the four holes. Make sure you cut the bottom of the birch bark piece evenly, so that the bouquet holder stands squarely on the table (see photograph 2).

* It is time to sew the overlapping pieces together. Loosen the juniper stick and make a row of small holes, one after the other, about 1 cm (about $\frac{3}{8}$ inch) away from the edge of the top flap (the pattern is marked where these holes will go). Use the smallest gouge. Reattach the juniper stick and mark the corresponding holes on the bark under the overlap, using a needle or a pencil. Loosen the juniper stick, make the holes in the underlying bark, reattach the juniper stick again, and start sewing, using backstitches. Start at the bottom. Attach the string well with a knot. At the top, you can fasten the string by sewing back into your stitches.

1.

2.

3.

5.

4.

*I have used small baby-food and jam jars in the examples above, but you can use any jar you want.*

* If you do not want to sew, you can glue down the overlapping flap. Make sure you first remove all the loose birch bark before you glue the pieces together. Hold the overlapping pieces together with paper clips or binder clips while the glue dries.

* The last thing you must do is to attach a piece of birch bark that will hold the glass jar in place. Cut out a 9½-inch-long by ¾-inch-wide birch-bark "ribbon." Bend it so it forms a U, place the glass inside the U (see photograph 3 on page 25), pull the birch-bark holder over the glass and the bark ribbon, and pull the ribbon tightly and bend it out over the edge of the vase. Fasten the bark ribbon to the bouquet holder with a small stapler.

## Instructions

The birch-bark vase cover (photographs 4 and 5 on page 25, and at right) really does bring nature indoors!

* For this project, the size of your birch bark will depend upon the size of the vessel you choose; there is no standard pattern. Measure the vase, add an inch to the top and make your own pattern from paper. In photograph 4 on page 25, you can see four larger holes punched in the bark for the juniper stick and the rows of smaller dots for sewing (if you choose to sew — an alternative is to use a strong, slow-drying glue, held together with clothespins until dry). There is no need for the birch-bark ribbon in this project.

# Birch-Bark Flower Basket

*You do not have to weave birch bark to make a basket. You can simply fold the bark piece to make a birch-bark basket. Use a black, rectangular container of hard plastic as a lining for it.*

## Materials

* paper
* pencil
* tape
* gouge
* cardboard
* birch bark
* hard plastic container
* slow-drying glue
* lightweight rope
* juniper sticks
* paper clips

## Tip

Birch bark is a living material that can buckle and twist in a warm, moist environment. Do not despair if this happens. Just heat the basket by holding it above a warm oven with the door open, and keep holding it in the shape you want it to be while it cools down.

## Instructions

Follow the instructions on page 24 for preparing the birch bark.

* To make a paper pattern, place the container on top of a piece of paper that's large enough to cover the plastic container. Bend the paper up along the long sides of the plastic container. Cut the paper along the long sides of the container at the same height as the container. If you are using a shallow container, cut the paper above the edge of the container. Make a cut in towards the container at each fold towards each short side. Fold the paper up along the short sides of the container, and cut the paper evenly with or above the edge at the same height as the long sides. Fold up all sides, including the flaps that project beyond the container on the long sides, on top of the short-side piece. Secure with a piece of tape. Make sure the top flaps do not overlap each other. They should leave a small space where the short side under shows.

* Make two holes in each flap that is overlapping the short sides. Mark the corresponding holes on the short sides. Make all the holes, but on the short sides the holes should be a little beyond the marks.

The distance between the holes on the inside edges is a little bigger than the distance between the holes on the outside. Doing this will make it easier to slide the locking juniper stick into place through the four holes, and the stick will not break as easily. If you want to run a rope around the basket (as shown in the first photograph at right), you have to make two additional holes on each long side at the same level as the holes on the short sides.

* Transfer the pattern onto smooth, stiff cardboard. Cut and punch out the holes with the gouge. Now you have a cardboard pattern that you can reuse.

* Place the long length of the pattern parallel with the stripes in the bark, trace, and cut. It is a good idea to make a small hole in the birch bark with the smallest gouge where the cut will terminate on the short sides. By doing this, you will avoid ripping the bark too far as you work with it. To keep the short sides from curling inwards, you should glue another piece of bark of the same size to the inside of the flap (you can see the second piece in the top photograph at right). Glue the white sides together, removing all loose bark before applying the glue. The holes in this piece should be slightly skewed in relationship to the short edges' holes, as mentioned above. This will help to keep the juniper stick from breaking.

* Prepare the juniper sticks (soak them in water for 24 hours, if they are dry and brittle) and attach them at the short sides.

# Birch-Twig "Nests"

*A birch-twig "nest" is a lovely way to display a floral bouquet. In the next few pages, I've included four designs that take advantage of the opportunities for seasonal bouquets. Making the nest is simple and requires few materials. After you've put it together, decorate it with greenery, pinecones, or even berries. A bouquet in a nest makes an ideal hostess gift and is perfect for any other occasion as well. Think about making several holders at one time, and put some away for later use.*

## Birch branches

Different parts of the birch tree are used in many of the decorations presented in this book. For example, birch branches, which are easily available, are strong and yielding, and by using them you can magically and economically create the most beautiful holders. However, keep in mind that you must work the branches (see "Softening branches" on page 14) before they dry out.

## Instructions

* Find a relatively long birch branch with several side branches. Strip off the leaves. Soften the branch, following the instructions on page 14. Make a circle using the main branch, and wrap the point of intersection with spool wire (see "Joining two branches" on page 14).

* Next, curve one of the side branches and fasten the loose end to the main branch at another point on the circle, to create an arc on the outside of the circle. Attach one side branch after another, so that you create one arc after another. The arcs can be on the same plane as the main circle, or they can be over or below it. Make sure that your construction is in balance. Add additional birch branches if necessary. You can use stem wire to attach the thinnest branches. As soon as you have completed the first circle (or after all the branches have been attached), you can make the handle for the construction. Attach three floral wires at different points on the main branch and gather them together in the middle of the inner circle, twisting them around each other until they're securely fastened. Cut the intertwined floral wires to make a handle of approximately 4 inches in length. Attach other materials as you wish.

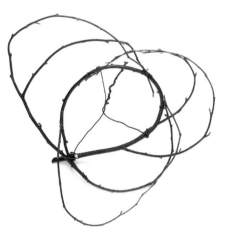

* The photograph at right shows a finished nest. For this holder, I used a larch branch with cones attached and a branch with lichen. Both branches are especially decorative and work well together to create balance. To complete my construction, I added some dwarf birch branches with fall colors, heather, and more lichen. The wire handle has been wrapped in floral tape.

The flowers which will decorate this holder will primarily be placed within the inner circle. Remember: the larger the circle, the more flowers you will need and the longer it will take to make the bouquet.

# Nest Bouquets

*It is the easiest thing in the world to put together a decorative bouquet when you have a birch nest at hand. You cannot fail! The birch nests you make will last for many years. Each season, you can create an entirely different bouquet from the season before, while still using the same nest. Once you've assembled the nest and bouquet, display the bouquet in your favorite vase, or you could even make a birch-bark skirt (see page 75) to place the flowers in and show off your arrangement to its best advantage.*

In the bouquet on the opposite page, I have included one elegant cymbidium orchid combined with greenery like Mexican heather (*Cuphea* hyssopifolia, a native plant of Texas and other arid, dry regions), Queen Anne's lace, yarrow, and bright red rose hips. The cymbidiums I sometimes use in my bouquets are not found in the wild, and I use them sparingly as they are so dramatic. There are wild-growing orchids in the U.S., found in California, Florida, New England and some northwestern states. California alone boasts more than 30 species, with the largest genus, *Piperia,* worth a closer look.

The photograph below is all greenery and is one of my favorites. The textures and shades of green are amazing, with small juniper branches, pinecones, green lichen, and Mexican heather (boxwood sprigs work as well).

## Materials
* one nest
* flowers and greenery
* vase in appropriate size for your flowers
* raffia

## Tips
Flowers and greenery can easily be placed between two arcs, which will help hold them in place.

If you want to use an orchid, lily, or another flower with a short stem, place it in a plastic test tube with a rubber top and put it into the decoration/bouquet.

For this nest of summer wildflowers (see opposite page), I chose juniper sprigs, lingonberry twigs, Mexican heather, lady's mantle, and seed heads from parsnip as greenery. Or try the berries from St. John's wort (Hypericum perforatum). St. John's wort grows wild throughout central Europe and the British Isles, but it has also been naturalized in many parts of the U.S. The white element is composed of daisies, yarrow, and sneezewort, also known as aster. To complete my color scheme, I have used Siberian poppies, red clover, and bluebells.

All these flowers grow in and around my home in Norway, but some can be found in the U.S., too. Siberian poppies are rare to find in the wild in North America, but there are plenty of substitutions. Icelandic poppies (Papaver croceum) can be seen growing in rocky areas from June to August. California poppies (Eschscholzia californica) have long stems and blue-green foliage. Colors range from deep yellow to red to white.

There are more than 18 species of bluebells in North America, and they can be found growing in forests, grasslands, mountainsides, along the ocean, and in brush areas. Red clover has naturalized and grows abundantly in North America, as well. Both are plentiful and pretty easy to spot.

## Instructions

* Hold the handle of the birch-branch nest in your hand and start by inserting juniper or some other greenery up against the birch circle. Then, create a "floor" made from evergreen twigs, to help keep flowers in position when you begin to put them in the nest in the next step. It's fine for the greens to stick out a little beyond the arcs of the birch branches.

* Next, place flowers into the construction. Start in the middle, using luxuriant greens (for example, lingonberry greenery) and a group of flowers of the same type. Keep filling in the nest with greenery and flowers, according to the season. You may want to have the tallest flowers in the center, and then the adjacent blooms can slope evenly downwards and out. As you add more flowers to the mix, your decoration will become full, and it will look very good from all sides. Create a pattern, and remember to use groupings and repetitions in your arrangement!

* Finish off the display by adding more greenery around the bouquet. As I mentioned previously, it's fine to have the greenery stick outside the nest, but it's also a good idea to create fullness down towards the area where you tied the bouquet, so that you conceal the opening of the vase as much as possible.

* When you have finished, wrap the tied up part with some raffia. Cut the flower stems with a sharp knife, and place them in a suitable vase.

34

# Bouquet Collar

*If you want to create an interesting and unique floral accessory, consider a bouquet collar, especially if you are using a tall vase. When a collar drapes down below the opening of a vase, the flowers sit just barely above it, creating a lovely sculptural look.*

## Instructions

Create a bouquet collar for a tall vase.

* Form a small circle from the main branch and tie it with spool wire.

* Attach the side branches to the small circle with stem wire, so that the arcs lie below it.

* Attach three floral wires to the small circle, gather them at the middle of the circle, and twist them together to form a handle. Cut the handle at an appropriate length, about 4 inches.

* Wrap the handle with floral tape.

* Place the bouquet collar on the opening of the vase, and then put one or more flowers, as well as some accompanying greenery, into the vase.

## Materials

* one thin, smooth birch branch with a few side branches
* floral wire
* spool wire, stem wire
* stem wire
* floral tape
* tall vase

To make the simple decoration above, I have only added airy lady's mantle and sun-yellow Siberian poppies. A few buds create textural variation and complete the composition! I bought the vase at Ikea and spray painted it black.

(opposite page)
See how effective it can be to decorate a birch nest with one large flower as the main attraction? Here, a dramatic purple Vanda orchid is the central focus among berry greens, green heather, and blooming white heather. Crab apples encircle the composition. They have been pinned and attached to birch twigs.

# Triangle-Shaped Collar

*Using small bunches of birch twigs, with or without early-spring catkins, you can easily conjure up a unique frame for your bouquet. Old, low-growing twigs work especially well.*

## Instructions

* Gather twigs into three bundles, using twigs of different lengths within each bundle. Make a triangle from the twig bundles by first fastening two bundles to each other with floral wire. Then attach the third bundle to the other two. Gather the floral wires to the center of the triangle. Twist them together to make a handle and cut them at an appropriate length, about 4 inches. Wrap floral tape around the handle to avoid rust when the collar is placed in water.

* With one hand, hold the triangular collar by the handle, and place the flowers, one after another, in the other hand, as if you were making an ordinary bouquet. Tie the stems with raffia. Put the entire display into a vase of your choice.

## Materials

* birch twigs
* floral wire
* floral tape
* raffia

## Tips

Make the length of the twig bundles about the length of your flower stems, so that you get harmonious proportions.

Twigs with lichen are particularly good to use for floral collars because of their beautiful texture.

*(opposite page)*
*This triangle-shaped collar is adorned with bluebells and lady's mantle and set in a birch-bark vase. It's stunning in its simplicity!*

39

## Materials

* floral wire
* 24-gauge spool wire
* stem wire
* floral tape
* hawthorn twigs, if desired

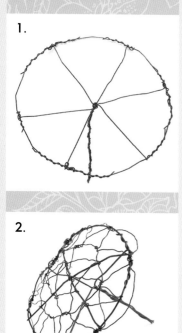

**1.**

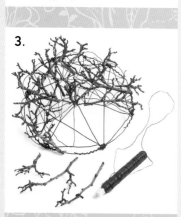

**2.**

**3.**

# Wire Bouquet Holders

*A wire bouquet holder, or "bouquet skeleton," offers lots of opportunities to create unique decorations. It can be reused, and it will change in character depending upon the season's flowers. In this way, the rhythms of the seasons can easily be brought into your home. The most practical wire designs are circles and heart shapes.*

## Instructions

Create a round wire bouquet holder.

* First, make a circle about the diameter of your finished bouquet, using the 24-gauge spool wire. Twist the ends securely together.

* Next, cut three more lengths of the wire, a little longer (maybe 2 inches) than the diameter of the circle. Attach one end of each at evenly spaced places around the circle, then stretch each wire to the opposite side through an imaginary center point. The "spokes" will have six points on the circle (see photograph 1).

* To make a handle, take two or three more lengths of spool wire and thread them down through the center of the circle. Twist the wires around each other and tighten them at the top with pliers. Finally, cover the handle with floral tape.

* Using more lengths of cut spool wire, attach the wire in between each of the six points, stretch it across the center point, wrap once, and continue to the other side.

40

* Cut stem wire lengths about the size of the circumference, and "weave" them laterally in between the spokes to create a wire mesh (see photograph 2 on the opposite page). Every time you go over or under a spoke, wrap the stem wire to create more points. You will want to create a mesh of small gaps, so that the flowers will stay in place as positioned.

* Create elongated arcs with spool wire on the underside of the rim, (see photograph 2). The arcs will be perfect for making a frame of green leaves or for keeping evergreen twigs in place.

* If you wish, attach small hawthorn twigs or other suitable twigs to the construction (see photograph 3 on the opposite page). Each little twig is fastened at two points with stem wire. You can choose if you want to cover the whole circle with them, or just the rim. When you have decorated the construction with twigs, the small, gnarled "twig heads" will poke up in between the flowers. The twigs will also help to support the flower heads.

## Tip

Holders for large flower heads can have larger holes than holders for smaller flower heads. For example, wood anemones and bluebells have small heads and thin stems, so if you select these flowers, it's to your advantage to use a weave with small holes in the construction.

## Tips

Using a large bouquet holder for small flowers will take a lot of work — create a holder that's the right size for the flowers you plan to include.

You can use many different flower types and colors for a round construction. Remember our design mantra: groupings and repetitions!

You can also make a circle form that is arched instead of flat. To do this, see the second bullet point under the instructions on page 40, and stretch the wires in an arc from one side to the other.

You can find examples of round bouquets that are made with wire skeletons on pages 43 and 45.

# Bouquets for Wire Holders

## Materials

* wire bouquet holder
* flowers
* greenery
* raffia
* vase

When you use a wire bouquet holder, it's wonderfully easy — and fun — to create an imaginative decoration for any occasion. The bouquet can be full and luscious one month, or stylish and refined the next. You can even make a wedding bouquet for your or a friend's wedding.

When you make a round bouquet, you can let your imagination run wild. Select several types of flowers, if you like, and make a pattern of textures and shapes. Remember that your design should include groups of the same flowers and colors that are repeated in various places in your arrangement. Berries and flowers with short stems must be pinned (see page 15). Finish off your bouquet with green leaves — for example, blueberry greenery or other greens with small leaves.

## Instructions

* Hold the wire bouquet holder in your hand, and place the flowers into the wire mesh. Begin in the middle, and then fill in flowers away from the center in all directions. You may end up with flowers in different layers.

* Finish off the bouquet by creating a green frame around the flowers. Place leaves, heather, or other greenery through the long loops around the edge of the bouquet holder.

*(opposite page)*
The photograph shows a simple, stylish bouquet made with wood anemones. Wood anemones are delightful spring flowers that can be found in the forests of eastern North America.

The flowers are placed in a round, arched wire construction decorated with hawthorn twigs. The wood anemones' leaves have been removed from the stems and placed into the elongated loops at the rim of the construction, to creating a green frame around the flowers.

* Wrap raffia around the tied stems, cut them at an angle, and place the entire decoration in a suitable vase. If you have made a wedding bouquet, use a birch-bark skirt for the stems, as described on page 75.

* You will find several examples of bouquets made with metal-wire holders on other pages in this book (pages 46, 48, and 49).

## Tip

The flowers should have small heads and be of the tender type. Wood anemones (without leaves) and Cuckoo flowers (*Cardamine* pratensis) — which can be found in or around swamps, wet woods, or wet fields — are lovely, as are all the other spring flowers with long stems.

*(opposite page)*
*A bouquet with flowers in all the colors of the rainbow: for this display, I chose flowers that are abundant in my native Oslo, as well as North America and Britain, such as white yarrow, bog star, yellow bird's-foot trefoil (Lotus corniculatus), poppies, yellow chamomile, orange rose hips, red rowan berries (mountain ash), bluebells, Queen Anne's lace, and parsnip. You can choose an equally diverse array from the wildflowers that grow in the woods and meadows in your area. All the flowers have been placed in a round wire holder, which has been covered with hawthorn twigs.*

# Heart-Shaped Wire Holders & Bouquets

*Instructions for making a heart-shaped bouquet holder are the same as for the round holder (see page 40). When you make a heart-shaped bouquet, it is best to use only one type of flower. If you use two types, one must be secondary to the other. A background of greenery always looks attractive. You can also finish your bouquet with greenery around the edges of the form.*

## Instructions

* Cut four even lengths of spool wire (the length will depend upon the final size of the heart), twist them together, and then bend the wires into a heart shape (see photograph 1, below).

* Stretch stem wires through an imaginary center point and attach them on the opposite side of the form. Start with a wire from the indentation at the top of the heart and string it to the bottom point of the heart. Then proceed to stretch wires from one long side of the heart to the other to make a wire mesh (see photograph 2).

* If you want to add a bouquet "handle," cut two more even lengths of spool wire, find a middle point, twist the wires around each other, and tighten them at the top with pliers. Wrap the handle with floral tape.

## Materials

* spool wire
* stem wire
* floral tape
* greening pins
* a variety of rose hips
* red berries on short stems

*(opposite page)*
*This eye-catching red heart is made from several varieties of rose hips, along with red berries intermixed with green lingonberry twigs. The rose hips must be pinned (see photograph above and see "Pinning" on page 15) and can be used to fill the entire form.*

1

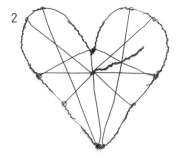

2

47

* Stretch a wire from each arch of the heart to the opposite long side, on both sides, and from the arches to the bottom point. Fasten wires from the indentation to each long side of the heart. The center point should be just below the point of the indentation, not midway between the indentation and the bottom point.

* Weave stem wires back and forth until you get the size of openings you want in your mesh.

The heart-shaped bouquet in the photograph on the left was created for a flower girl. (See "Bouquets for Wire Holders" on page 42 for decorating instructions). The birch-bark skirt is explained on page 75.

*Tip*
I use one type of flower because I believe a unified look is best when creating this arrangement — the focus should be on the shape of the heart.

# Wreaths

*Corky fungi (Polyporaceae) have beautiful colors and shapes. They can be used to create a rougher and more rustic expression for your decoration.*

*Corky fungi and conifer cones must be pinned (see "Pinning" on page 15).*

# Spruce Wreath

*When you make a flower wreath, you must fasten the flowers to a base. There are several materials to choose from for your base: straw, floral foam, or spruce. My personal favorite is the spruce wreath.*

## Instructions

* Pick long, chubby, symmetrical spruce branches, 24–32 inches long. Place a branch partially on top of another and wrap them together with spool wire. Continue to place branches on top of each other, slightly offset. Wrap. You will get a chubby, round garland.

* Bend the garland to form a circle, overlap the ends, and attach by wrapping with wire. Fasten the wire. Wrap extra well to ensure that the wreath will not unravel if you, by accident, should cut the spool wire. Bend and adjust the wreath until it makes a symmetrical ring. If the wreath has patchy areas with uneven thickness, wrap small bunches of spruce at the uneven spots. Wrap the wreath so tightly that it maintains its shape.

* Attach juniper branches at the bottom edge of the wreath where it meets your work surface, both on the outside and the inside of the ring. Cut long or short branches at an angle, tuck them on an angle into the wreath, and fasten them with greening pins. You can also attach a few juniper sprigs on the top of the wreath.

* In addition to small flower bouquets you can attach other materials from nature to the wreath: roots, twig bunches, stones, moss and lichen, corky fungi, and pinecones. Fasten all materials with greening pins.

  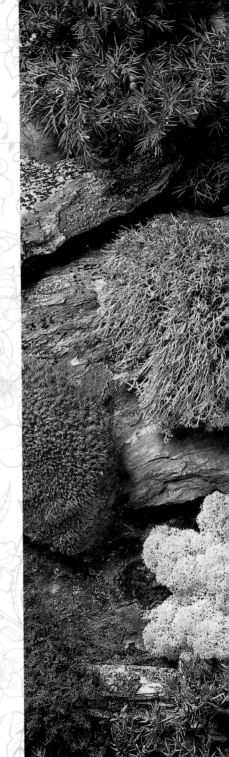

## A Wreath Base Made from Spruce Branches

When you use a straw wreath base, you must pin or attach the flowers with wires to the base. Many wildflowers must be in water the whole time to keep them from withering. Consequently, you cannot pin them or attach them with wires. When using a floral-foam wreath, you can decorate with flowers that have a stiff stem and are able to hold water for a while. Cultivated flowers and some wildflowers fall into this category. However, many wildflowers have thin, soft stems that are difficult to push into a floral-foam wreath. This is when the spruce wreath comes into play. The wildflowers can be placed in their own water containers (see "Water containers," page 15) into this type of wreath, and consequently will last a lot longer.

A wreath made from spruce branches has other advantages when compared to the ones made from floral foam or straw. You can make it exactly as large as you wish. You can change the composition of colors and flowers many times without destroying the base. (A floral-foam wreath is perforated and ruined after one use.) The spruce wreath does not leak water, and it is a lot less expensive — free, actually, if you pick the branches yourself.

# Spruce Wreath with Flowers

*Let the heady scent of high-summer flowers enhance your home. Create your own version of a luxuriant summer meadow on a beautiful wreath. Without doubt, the decoration will bring a smile to those who visit. When you decorate a wreath, it is just like painting with flowers.*

A wreath made from spruce branches is a very good base for a flower wreath. It works well for wildflowers in summer and for cultivated flowers throughout the rest of the year. When you are creating your wreath, it is important to look for harmony and beauty, balance and structure. It is a good idea to have your bouquets ready to be attached before you start to decorate your wreath.

## Instructions

* Make individual flower bouquets with one or two flowers and finish them off with something green, like heather or leaves, around the edges (see photograph on page 57). Only use one type of flower in each bouquet. Unremarkable flowers such as lady's mantle and Queen Anne's lace can be successfully mixed into a bouquet as fillers. Cut the stems and stick each small bouquet through the hole in a test tube's rubber top. The test tube should already be filled with water. You can enlarge the rubber top's hole with a knife if it is too small.

## Materials

* spruce wreath
* plastic test tubes with rubber tops
* greening pins
* flowers and natural materials

*(opposite page)*
*Small bouquets are wrapped in bundles and ready for wreath making. The flowers featured here include marsh marigolds (Caltha palustris), easily found in wet areas in North America, and cowslips (Primula veris), lovely spring flowers that are abundant in Britain but not so easy to find in the northern hemisphere. North American substitutes include celandine poppies (Stylophorum diphyllum), about 12 inches tall with showy yellow flowers, which are commonly found in the midwestern states. Golden ragwort (Packera aurea), found in eastern North America, has bright yellow flowers. The other flowers include buttercups, wood anemones, lily of the valley, violets, and blueberry-bush twigs.*

Place a small amount of moss on top of the rubber top before you push the bouquet into the plastic test tube. The moss will hide the rubber top if the flowers' leaves do not conceal it well enough.

If you want the wreath to last a long time, you must make sure to refill the test tubes with water. Lift the top off and use a spray bottle to refill.

* Stick the test tubes into the spruce wreath as desired, creating a pattern. Group the flowers. You may want to place several bouquets of the same type of flower next to each other. By working this way, you create a calmer impression that is more pleasing to the eye. (Your eyes find resting points when the fields of color are larger.) If you have trouble pushing the test tubes into the wreath, you can create an opening by sticking a pencil or screwdriver into the desired place. It is very easy to change your composition if you do not like it. Just pull out the test tubes with flowers and rearrange.

* In addition to the bouquets, you can fasten other natural materials to the wreath. Flowers and greenery that are not dependent upon a constant supply of water can be attached directly to the wreath, with or without greening pins.

# Birch-Twig Wreath with Flowers

*Place an airy wreath formed from birch branches directly on a table. It will work very well as an unusual but charming flower "vase."*

### Instructions

* Soften the branches, as described on page 14.

* Start by using one branch to make a circle as large as you want, and attach the branches with spool wire to each other where they cross, as described on page 14. The remaining part of the main branch is then attached once or several times to this circle, as needed. Keep the spool wires long, so that you can use them to continuously wrap new branches as you lay the branches on top of each other.

(see page 14)

## Materials

* many birch branches
* spool wire
* stem wire
* test tubes
* flowers
* branches from green dogwood or similar

*(opposite page)*
*Most flowers are suitable for this birch-twig wreath, but flowers with curvy stems look the best. Ranunculus (pictured here at different lengths and growth stages) have curvy stems that fit well with the style of the wreath. The stems have almost the same green color as the green dogwood branches.*

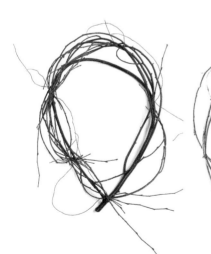

Any branch can be used, with or without side branches. It is preferable to use long branches. Just make sure that you are able to bend them.

The birch-twig wreath is also great to hang on the wall as an Advent calendar before Christmas. If you make it sturdy enough, it can carry the weight of 24 small surprises. A lighter version can easily be hung on a door. Decorate it with a bow made from birch bark or textiles and some seasonal ornaments.

Orchids, or other flowers with large heads, look great on this wreath.

* Stick the thicker end of a new branch through the branch below until it hits the work surface, and attach it at a new place. Secure several new branches in the same way by establishing several points of attachment. As you go, attach side branches to the established points of attachment or to new points, either with spool wire or stem wire (for the thinnest branches). Make sure that your arches have a nice shape. Do not attach the branches at too many points. Some side branches can be secured across the long direction of the wreath, to provide more support for the test tubes. Place the test tubes last. Side branches can also be wrapped around other branches.

* The wreath should be chubby, so you need to use quite a lot of branches. When you have achieved the desired size, you can finish off by weaving in, for example, red or green dogwood branches in elegant arches. This finishing touch really sets off the wreath.

* At this point, you can place test tubes in between the branch arches. Secure the test tubes with stem wire as needed.

## Materials

* lots of lilies of the valley
* greenery with small leaves (for example, blueberry-bush sprigs)
* wreath-shaped wet floral foam
* stem wire
* spiked candleholders, if desired

## Tip

Since the lily of the valley stem is rather stiff, and you are not going to create a pattern, you can, preferably, use a floral-foam ring instead of a wreath made from evergreens.

*(opposite page)*
*A romantic and heavenly scented table is set with candlelit wreaths and balls of lilies of the valley. Place cards are made from birch branches, birch bark, and rowan flowers (see page 93). The candles have been placed in tin candleholders with long spikes.*

# Lily of the Valley Wreath

*Lilies of the valley have a wonderful scent. Pick buckets full and fill your home with the heavenly perfume. Use them to enhance your spring party as well as your everyday life.*

*Blueberry bushes are newly sprung out and are intensely green when the lilies of the valley bloom. They work very well as a filler for the wreath. The wreaths are gorgeous as decorations on a table. If you add lit candles, the expression becomes even more romantic and magical. When you use candles, place them in metal candleholders with spikes, and set them into the floral foam.*

## Instructions

* Moisten the wet floral-foam ring (see page 15).
* Cut the stems at an angle. Stick short blueberry sprigs, or similar sprigs, at an angle and place them densely into the ring, always in the same direction. Use small lily of the valley leaves in between the sprigs to create variety.

* Then fill the wreath with short bouquets of about five lilies of the valley each. Cut them at an angle and stick them into the floral foam without tying them together.

### Lily of the Valley Ball

These beautiful balls can be used as decorations by themselves, but they look especially luxuriant when placed on a table set for a party, together with lily of the valley wreaths with candles. Use suitable dishes under the balls and distribute them around the table. Use the same method for making the balls as you did for making the wreath; just use a wet floral-foam ball instead of a ring.

# Four Seasonal Wreaths

*These wreaths have been decorated to reflect the different seasons of the year, using flowers and natural materials that are typical of each season.*

## Spring Is Finally Here

Bunches of purple liverleaf play the main roles in this wonderful wreath, seen on the opposite page. They are accompanied by other "wild" materials, such as juniper twigs, spruce cones, larch cones, corky fungi, different lichen, newly sprung leaves from the lime tree, and berry-bush sprigs. In early spring, wildflowers are few and far between, so white cymbidium orchids, green hydrangeas, and kangaroo paws (*Anigozanthos*) finish off the composition.

## High Summer

All the beautiful summer flowers are concentrated in one wreath, in the photograph at right. You may use white daisies, Queen Anne's lace, cinquefoil, yellow globeflower, buttercup, bird's-foot trefoil, toadflax, yellow chamomile, lady's mantle, bloody cranesbill, red clover, blue bellflower, and common bugloss (*Anchusa* officialis) for your wreath. To complement all the flowers, use a lot of blueberry sprigs, juniper, and some raspberry leaves.

*(above)*
*This is the same wreath base as the spring wreath on page 67, but we have substituted three orchids and corky fungi with some luxurious, golden ranunculus.*

## Wonderful Fall

As fall sets in, you can compose a wreath imbued with the mood and feelings of the season (see photographs at left, top and bottom). A wreath can decorate your table for a fall party, showing off brilliantly the blushing colors of nature, along with some cultivated flowers. The summer flowers have withered, and rose hips, berries, and fruit create the colors for the fall wreath. In addition to a rustic mixture of evergreen cones, corky fungi, lichen, and moss, I have decorated the wreath with rose hips, crab apples, and berry-bush sprigs. The main flowers are cymbidium orchids, Amazon lilies, and hydrangeas, along with waxplant, euphorbia, sea holly (*Eryngium*), and cone-bush cones (*Leucadendron*).

## Beautiful Winter

There are not many plants to be found outside in the middle of winter. But what you do have is texture, and lots of it! It is great to have a supply of coniferous cones, corky fungi, and various types of lichen that you have gathered earlier. The additional materials used in this wreath (see opposite page) have been bought in stores, and they consist of Vanda orchids, anemones, irises, African violets, cymbidium orchids, waxplants, ranunculus, euphorbia, viburnum, snowball bushes, seed crowns from silkweed, mimosas, and tropical plants like cone bush, berzelia, and albiflora.

# Wedding Celebrations

# Wedding Flowers

*Flowers are always present at weddings and at other important occasions. It is especially meaningful if you spend some time and effort in making the decorations yourself, using seasonal flowers. Why not ask the maid of honor or the future bride (or the groom) to create the wedding bouquet? Such a bouquet would reflect the bride's personality and her love of nature in a very special way. Help her make it exuberant or simple, and it will be just perfect.*

A bouquet can have many shapes: round, heart shaped, teardrop shaped, or elongated. For instructions on how to make wire forms in the shape of a heart, or round ones with or without hawthorn twigs, see pages 47 and 40. A birch-bark skirt (see on page 24) is an excellent accessory for a wildflower bouquet and lends a handcrafted touch to any wedding that features handmade decorations.

*In the photograph above, and on page 68, the orchids have been substituted with blue common bugloss, a lovely plant found growing all summer in meadows. It too has long stems, and like black hay (Medicago lupulina), lovely accent that hangs and elongates the bouquet. The flower girl and the wedding party can carry miniature versions of the bride's bouquet.*

*(opposite page)*
*This heart-shaped bouquet is formed by a wire frame (see page 47) that gives wedding bouquets a whole new look. Queen Anne's lace creates a dense pillow where the phalaenopsis orchids rest. Sometimes I use "store-bought" flowers when I want a special look, and white orchids qualify perfectly for this occasion. Some of the long, hanging stems are black hay or black medic, an easy-to-find meadow weed with long, 20-inch stems. It has small, yellow flowers grouped in tight bunches.*

# Wedding Bouquet with a Birch-Bark Skirt

*What kind of a wedding bouquet you choose depends upon your wishes and flower choices. There are many suggestions in this book that you can consider. Regardless of what you choose, a wildflower bouquet needs water, so I had to come up with a special solution to this problem. My specialty is wedding bouquets with birch-bark skirts. Below are instructions on how to make one.*

## Instructions

* When you have finished binding the bouquet with raffia, cut the stems at an angle, keeping them somewhat short, and wrap them in moist paper towels. Cover the moist towels with black plastic.

* A birch-bark skirt is fitted by placing an adequately large sheet of birch bark at an angle beyond and overlapping around the black plastic (or you could use the pattern on page 136). Roughly cut the bark as you hold it in the shape of a vase around the bouquet, and mark where the locking stick will be placed. Make four holes with the gouge (see a detailed description on page 24).

* Tighten the birch bark again around the plastic and stick a juniper stick through the four holes. Trim the bottom of the bark so that the plastic is covered and the bouquet can stand by itself. Make sure that there is a harmonious relationship between the bouquet and the birch-bark skirt. If the birch-bark skirt has been fastened correctly, the bouquet will not fall out.

## Materials

* raffia
* wedding bouquet
* birch bark (or ribbons, or decorative paper)
* a thin juniper stick
* paper towels
* black plastic
* gouge/drill

*The birch-bark skirt above, has been sized to fit the bouquet, and it covers the black plastic (which covers the moist paper towels wrapped around the stems).*

*(opposite page)*
*This wedding bouquet has been made using a round, arched wire form. It is composed of globe-mallow (sphaeralcea), buttercup, daisies, Queen Anne's lace (cow parsley), yarrow, lady's mantle, and forget-me-nots.*

You can make the bouquet the day before the wedding. If you do, you may place the whole birch-bark skirt under water and dry it out in time for the ceremony. Add water to the paper towels, rewrap them in plastic, and give the bouquet to the bride just before she will walk down the aisle. Moisten the paper towels again before the bouquet is placed on the table.

## Tips

A simpler method of creating a birch-bark skirt is to wrap a sheet of birch bark around the plastic and fasten it with a special string.

If you do not have birch bark, you can wrap beautiful ribbons or decorative paper around the plastic, but they won't be as sturdy.

*(opposite page)*
*A lovely bride with her globe mallow, daisy, and buttercup bouquet — perfect for a summer wedding.*

## Materials

* silver birch branches (remove big leaves)
* string of pearls plant
* feathers
* lichen
* spool wire
* stem wire
* floral tape
* flowers

*(opposite page)*
*This wedding bouquet is made from drooping branches from the silver birch tree, string of pearls, feathers, lichen, phalaenopsis orchids, and Amazon lilies.*

# Silver-Birch Bouquet

*This bouquet is an irresistible combination of rough branches, small feathers, and lichen, paired with store-bought orchids and lillies. If you live in the southern or southwestern U.S., there are some lovely wildflower substitutions, such as mariposa lily (Calochortus leichtlinii), found in California's Sierra Nevada mountains, Texas, Arizona, etc. Another Texas wildflower (also in Florida), is the white prickly poppy (Argemone albiflora), a gorgeous flower on a long stem, but with hazardous spiny leaves. As with many poppies, you must sear the end of the stem, so the bloom lasts longer. You can make the bouquet holder several days ahead and add the flowers the day of the celebration.*

## Instructions

* Pick long, elegant silver-birch branches with side branches. If silver-birch branches are not available, you might try young weeping-willow branches.

* Place two or several branches next to each other. Tie them together with spool wire at the thick end to form a handle (see photograph at left, top), and wrap the handle with spool wire, then floral tape.

* Make a pleasing form by weaving the side branches to each other. Create space and depth by forming arches and lines. Using side branches, weave the branches into each other, crisscrossing as you work "downwards" using stem wire. If you wish, you can attach additional branches (see photograph at left, bottom).

* Attach small feathers to the branches, preferably white or brown and white. A copper-colored stem wire will look very nice. Then add the lichen and weave in lengths of the string of pearls (Senecio rowleyanus). The "pearls" last quite a while without water and can be found growing in the southern states of the U.S., but they create such an elegant look that you may want to purchase a plant for your home.

* Wrap brown floral tape around the flower stems and attach them with stem wire to the birch branches.

78

# Myrtle Headpiece

## Materials
* myrtle sprigs
* spool wire
* stem wire
* floral tape

*Myrtle (Myrtus communis) was a sacred flower of the goddess of beauty and love, Aphrodite. It symbolizes fertility and eternal love. Although myrtle is hard to find in North America, there are substitutions, such as boxwood or sprigs from other ornamental garden shrubs.*

## Instructions

* Twist several spool wires together, keeping the length a little longer than the circumference of the wearer's head. Make a loop in one end.

* Using additional wires, shape the points for the crown or the tiara (see photograph at right, top). Fasten them by wrapping the wires onto the main wire. A crown has points of the same height all around the circumference. For a tiara, you would make the center point highest and then taper the other points down; there are not any points in the back.

* Wrap floral tape around all the wires.

* Next, attach myrtle sprigs with stem wire so closely together that you cannot see the floral-tape-covered wires. Start at the points and work your way downwards. When the points are done, cover the main wire with myrtle sprigs. Adjust the size of your crown or tiara by pulling one end of the wire through the loop, tightening, and "locking."

(above, bottom)
A heart made with myrtle sprigs and placed on a table creates a romantic mood at the wedding feast.

(opposite page)
A beautiful bride is even lovelier with a myrtle crown. You can also use sprigs from bushes with similar shiny leaves.

# Wildflower Headpiece

*If you are thinking of wearing a floral headpiece on your wedding day, more often than not, the offerings are constructions made of silk flowers. They can be quite beautiful, but if you want to personalize a headpiece and really make it yours, why not make one? And make a few for your wedding party? The possibilities are endless.*

Be aware that many of the early-summer flowers are fragile and will wither very fast; for example, bluebells, wood anemones, and violets do not stay fresh long. High-summer flowers (thistles, tansy, daisies, and red clover) are longer lasting. Buds are excellent, and they often have beautiful colors and textures. Berries and seed crowns are equally nice. Some types of heather are long lasting. Experiment and find out! Place your chosen plants in water a whole night before you use them.

## Instructions

* Attach several floral wires to each other, ending up with a length that is a little longer than the circumference of the wearer's head. Make a loop at one end. Cover the wire with floral tape. Do not cover the loop.

* Attach heather, greenery, and wildflowers (in small groups of little flowers with short stems) to the wire that is covered with floral tape by using stem wire. You may prefer to make a series of small bouquets and add those (see photo at right). Make the wreath as chubby as you like by adding more plants.

## Materials

* long-lasting summer flowers
* heather
* greenery sprigs
* floral wire
* stem wire
* floral tape

*(opposite page)*
*This headpiece consists of the common northern dock, scentless chamomile, woolly burdock, thistle, yarrow, red clover, and yellow chamomile. You can also add more flowers: sneezewort, daisies, white clover, valerian buds, meadowsweet, tansy, berry-bush sprigs, and seed crowns from mustard plants.*

* When you are done attaching the flowers onto the wire, secure the stem wire you used to attach flowers. Pull the end of the floral wire through the loop and fasten the wire, after you have sized the headpiece to the wearer's head.

## Tip

If you find that you have to make the headpiece in advance of the time you will use it, keep it in the refrigerator, lightly wrapped in moist paper towels, and spray it often.

## Materials

* plastic test tube with a rubber top
* long, thin pieces of birch bark
* safety pin or a specialty pin
* glue gun
* greenery
* flowers
* twigs (optional)

*(opposite page)*
*This boutonniere uses yellow summer flowers, bluebells, white sweet clovers, Queen Anne's lace, and lady's mantle leaves placed in a plastic test tube that's been covered with a piece of birch bark.*

# Boutonnieres

*It is a wedding tradition that the groom, best man, and father of the bride wear a flower decoration, a boutonniere, on their left lapel at the festivities. Of course, others who are close to the bride and groom may also wear one. There really are no rules.*

## Instructions

* Glue a safety pin or a specialty pin onto a plastic test tube that has a rubber top. Wrap and glue very thin, ribbon-like pieces of birch bark around the test tube and pin (see photograph at left).

* Make a small bouquet of flowers and greenery, placing one green leaf in the back of the flowers as background.

* Cut the flower stems at an angle and push the stems through the rubber top. Make a larger hole in the rubber top if you need to.

Flowers that do not need much water (carnations and roses, for example) can be used without being placed in water. Wrap brown floral tape around the stem, which should be about 2–2⅜ inches long, and wrap the safety pin or the specialty pin also. Then cover the tape by wrapping a colored spool wire (copper is nice) tightly around the floral tape. Finish by sticking the ends of the wires into the flower. If you are using drooping

**Tip**

The boutonniere flowers should complement the flowers in the wedding bouquet, except if you are using white carnations.

silver-birch branches for the wedding bouquet (see page 78), a boutonniere of the same material would be perfect. Make a generous circular shape from drooping silver-birch branches and tie them together with spool wire. Attach a safety pin or a specialty pin to the circle and place a flower that does not need water (for example, an orchid) in the middle (see photograph, opposite).

*(opposite page)*
*Pictured is an elegant and unique boutonniere composed of drooping silver-birch branches, string of pearls, a phalaenopsis orchid, and feathers.*

# Wedding-Party Flowers

For a young child, to be a member of a wedding party is fun, exciting, and maybe a bit nerve-racking! The flower girl carries a miniature version of the bride's bouquet, and the ring bearer either wears a boutonniere similar to the groom's or attaches a boutonniere to a staff that he carries down the aisle.

Above is a small heart bouquet made from buttercups and Queen Anne's lace.

This wedding bouquet has a birch-bark skirt, which conceals the plastic and moist paper towels around the stems (see page 75).

(opposite page)
A thoughtful flower girl is standing in a field of daisies. Her bouquet has been made using a small, round wire bouquet holder and is composed of bird's-foot trefoil, meadow saxifrage, Queen Anne's lace, and forget-me-nots.

A happy ring bearer is holding his decorated staff, awaiting the wedding ceremony. Thistle, common bugloss, and larch leaves have been placed in a plastic test tube covered with birch bark and attached to the staff about 4–6 inches from the top. Ground elder is blooming in the background.

# Reception Place Cards with Birch Holders

*A place card and pedestal holder made from birch bark, and a small branch of birch, are just the things to create a harmonious whole when you have used other natural materials as table decor. They also make memorable favors for your guests to take home.*

## Materials

* birch branches, about 1⅛–1⅝ inches in diameter
* birch bark
* waterproof calligraphy pen
* drill
* small saw
* vise

Not all flowers will work equally well as decorations for place cards. They should not be large, and they should be able to look good all evening without water. Some flowers that will work well are: small daisies, clover, golden root, tansy, thistles, pin-cushion flowers, and mountain-ash berries. During winter, you can use African violets, hydrangeas, and St. John's wort berries. Experiment!

(opposite page)
The place cards and pedestal holders enhance a party table decorated with a lily of the valley arrangement (see page 64). These pedestal place-card holders have been decorated with a juniper sprig and berry flowers.

## Instructions

**The pedestal:**

* Cut the branches into pedestal holders about 1⅛–1⅝ inches long, using pruning shears or a saw.
* Set the pedestal holders into a vise and make angled cuts, creating slits about ⅜–½ inch deep.
* Drill two holes in the holder in front of the angle cut, one from the left at an angle towards the right, and one from the front down and towards the back. The first hole should be mostly horizontal.

**The place card:**

* The birch-bark place card can be punched out with a die cutter, a punch, or cut with scissors into a circle, about 2⅜ inches in diameter.
* Write the guest's name on the birch-bark card with a waterproof pen and place it in the angled slit. You can make a little fold at the bottom of the card if the slit is too wide, or you may use a small twig in the slit behind the card to hold it in place.
* Stick a juniper sprig in the horizontal hole and a flower in the hole at the front.

## Tips

If you are going to cut many pedestal holders, it would be more efficient to use an electric saw. Cut the branches into lengths of about 20–23 inches. Set the saw in such a manner that you can make angled cuts by holding the branch at an angle above the rotating saw blade. Make angled cuts at both ends of all the branches.

Readjust the saw so that you can cut off the ends of the branch into pieces of the right length. The pedestals should to be about 1⅛–1⅝ inches in length.

Then readjust the saw again and make new cuts at an angle into both ends of the birch branch. Repeat the process, but stop sawing when the birch branch has become short (watch your fingers).

*This place card has been elegantly decorated with a juniper sprig and a single African violet.*

# Reception-Table Flower Arrangements

*It is not by accident that flowers always have decorated our tables — their scent and beauty create a perfect atmosphere. A traditional table arrangement is typically composed of flowers placed into floral foam that is shaped like a fan. Adding an arched branch to this traditional arrangement elevates it, literally, to another plane. By using simple materials, you can make a rather ordinary decoration "fly," and the atmosphere around the table will also, hopefully, rise to new levels.*

## Traditional Fan-Shaped Arrangement

Use long, slim, and elegant juniper branches in the long direction, and shorter branches in the short direction. Berry-bush branches or other greenery with small leaves are ideal for creating color variations and texture. Use what is available during the different seasons. Especially during summer, there is an abundance of greenery to choose from. Blueberry-bush branches that are newly sprung out have a lovely, green spring color, as do heather, the mountain-ash berry bush, the raspberry bush, and many others.

## Instructions

* Place wet floral foam into a suitable low dish or container. Let the floral foam project at least ¾ inch above the dish. Begin by placing the greenery that will project out over the table. When you are done, the highest point of the arrangement should be in the middle, and it should taper off at an angle and out.

* When most of the greenery is in place, begin placing the flowers by using the buds and smallest flowers towards the top and furthest away from the floral foam. Place the largest flower heads closer to the floral foam. Start in the middle and work your way down and out. Gather the flowers in groups. Do not mix too many colors or types of flowers in one arrangement. Think about lines and creating a harmonious expression.

* If you want to add a branch arch over the arrangement, you could stick the branches into each short side of the floral foam and tie them together in an arch over the arrangement using stem wire. Add branches as needed to balance the arch.

## Flat Flower Arrangement

Flat flower arrangements look very attractive at the end of large banquet tables set in a "U" or "E" configuration. To make the arrangement, start by tying together a bed of beautiful juniper branches (preferably branches with green berries attached). Make several bouquets with one type of flower in each and stick them into test tubes with rubber tops. Attach the test tubes to the juniper branches. The tallest flower bouquets are attached first, and then continue to attach bouquets in order of size. Add more juniper branches as needed. Wrap a decorative rope around the end of the bouquet if you want to.

This flat flower arrangement consists of juniper branches, tansy, bluebells, moutain-ash berries, and wild celery.

99

## Materials

* wet floral foam
* greenery
* juniper twigs
* berry-bush branches
* leaves
* flowers

*Above is a small, simple, front-facing flower arrangement featuring cowslips in the main role, and enhanced by juniper twigs and branches from a newly sprung-out chestnut tree in supporting roles.*

*(opposite page)*
*By placing a self made arrangement on the stairs at your entrance you will make guests feel extra welcome and the arrangement will help set a festive mood even before you open the door. This front facing flower arrangement consists of juniper branches and other greenery as the base. Purple Viper's bugloss and dark mullein create the height, yellow chamomile, red clover, daisies, common bugloss, meadowsweet buds and ground elders create fullness.*

# Front-Facing Flower Arrangements

*A front-facing flower arrangement quite clearly has a front and a back. It looks very fitting on a table up against a wall.*

If you are going to make a very large front-facing flower arrangement, you should use special floral foam that already is set in a plastic container. You can buy it at a floral shop or a craft store. Let the long side be the front. You could also, if you want, fill a large dish with floral foam and let it stick an inch or so above the edge of the dish. Secure the floral foam to the dish by using floral-foam prongs, which are glued to the dish with hot glue or waterproof clay. You can also buy these materials at floral shop or a craft store.

## Instructions

* Cut the branches at an angle before you stick them into well-moistened floral foam. Place taller branches towards the back of the floral foam and shorter branches out to the sides and towards the front.

* Add other greenery until you have a luxurious composition.

* Arrange the flowers as you wish, but remember to make groups and repetitions. If the flowers need more water than the floral foam supplies, or the stems are not long enough to be placed directly into the foam, you can place them into test tubes with rubber tops. You have to pin (see page 15) the test tubes before you place them into the floral foam. Cover exposed floral foam or test tubes with moss, lichen, or leaves.

A small front-facing flower arrangement does not need more than a third of a floral foam block. That size will fit very well into the birch-bark basket that is described on page 28. You can, of course, place the floral foam in any dish or container.

### Tip

If you want to make an arch to extend over the arrangement, or to give it a little extra height, you can choose to use Chinese-lantern branches, rose-hip branches, branches with larch cones, branches from cherry trees that are just about to spring out or that have newly sprung out, mountain-ash berry branches, raspberry branches, or similar branches.

# Twigs & Sprigs

# Conifer-Cone "Vases"

*I have so many memories about conifer cones. As a child growing up in Norway, I often made conifer-cone animals, people, and birds. I heard stories about distant and near relatives who collected conifer cones to make fires to keep warm. I, also, use conifer cones, but perhaps in a non-traditional way. The result, though, "warms" the environment wherever they are placed, whether on a fireplace mantel or on a table.*

## Instructions

* Strip large pinecones to get many scales. Cut the scales at an angle at the "bottom." Make the scales pointed as much as possible, to avoid crumbling the floral foam when you stick them into the foam.

* Cut the top off the floral foam, if you are going to use one that is in the shape of a cone. If you are going to use one that is shaped like a ball, you should cut a slice off the bottom, so that the ball will sit flat on a surface. Press the water container (test tube) into the top of the dry floral foam. The size of the water container should correspond to the height of the floral foam — the higher the floral foam, the larger the water container.

* Dip the pointed (cut) end of each pine scale into the melted glue and stick it quickly into the floral foam. If you are slow, the glue will dry before you place the scales. Start at the top by the water container and work your way downwards in a spiral, placing the pine scales rather tightly. When you are done, fill in any unwanted openings with the smallest scales.

## Materials

* pinecones
* dry floral foam
* hot-melt pan glue
* glue pan
* glass or plastic test tubes
* flowers
* shears

## Tip

Large floral-foam pieces can be carved into any shape you want. If you make a larger shape, you can place more than one test tube into the floral foam.

(opposite page)
The photograph shows conifer-cone vases with wood anemones. The vases are made with cone- and ball-shaped floral foam and pinecone scales from the eastern white pine.

# Hair Cap Moss Wreath

A round wreath made from hair cap moss (Polytrichum *commune*) can be used as a mat on a table under vases or candlesticks. As it dries, the moss color changes from green to a beautiful, brown-red color. You can find hair cap moss growing in chubby, pillow-like forms in marshes and other moist areas. Pick only the extra-long bear moss for this project.

## Materials

* hair cap moss
* floral wire
* spool wire

*(opposite page)*
*A newly made hair cap moss wreath makes a luxurious statement in any decoration. In this picture, the birch-bark vase (see page 24) fits just right into the middle of the wreath. The birch nest in the birch-bark vase has been decorated with flowers reflecting a winter theme. I used heather, berry-bush greenery, anemones, tulips, snap dragons, euphorbia buds, and lady's mantle to create a lively and nuanced bouquet.*

## Instructions

* Clean the moss free of debris. Make moss bunches of about 40–50 stems, making sure that you have the same number of stems in each bunch. Cut all the moss bunches at the same length, about 10 inches.

* Make a circle using heavier floral wire, twisting several wires together if necessary.

* Tie the moss bunches to the wire ring, as shown in the drawings (opposite page). Place the bundles closely together and tighten the knots well, so that the moss will stay in place as it dries. Fasten the end of the last moss bundle with spool wire.

## Tip

Keep the hair cap-moss wreath out of direct sunlight, and it will stay green longer.

A bunch of
hair cap moss

A circle-shaped
floral wire

# Artistic Twig Vase

*Create a unique, artistic vase by gathering a number of twigs of different lengths and arranging them around glass test tubes.*

(opposite page)
*We have decorated the twig vase with cerise-red anemones. The stems are supported by climbing-hydrangea seed crowns. Surrounding the twig vase is a wreath of hair cap moss, which has dried but still green (see page 110 for instructions).*

## Materials

* twigs in an assortment of sizes
* rubber band
* rope
* glass test tubes
* flowers

## Instructions

* Collect many twigs of different colors. The twigs should be rather straight and without much side growth. Red and green dogwood branches, linden, and maple-tree branches work very well. Use only the part of the twig that has a thickness of about ⅜ inch. Cut the twigs into your chosen length, but not all of them with exactly the same length. Gather a large bunch of twigs and hold them together with a strong rubber band. You could also use sturdy black elastic. (However, you must sew this elastic together before you make the bundle of twigs.)

* When your twig bundle is ready, you can stick, for example, three glass test tubes into the middle of the bundle. The rubber band will hold it all together. Then wrap a rope several times around the sticks to conceal the rubber band. Test tubes that are 4–4¾ inches work well for the shorter twig vases. Large twig vases made from long, thicker branches need test tubes that are 7¾–12 inches long.

112

* As the twigs dry and shrink, you can add additional twigs to your vase or tighten the rope. You may also choose to dry the twigs beforehand. However, the twigs look the best and create the nicest decorations when they are fresh!

If you want to create volume or need to support the flower stems, you can use, for example, baby's breath or climbing-hydrangea seed crowns and place them into the test tubes before the flowers.

## Tips

Fresh twigs have a lot of moisture in them. If you use these, you must be aware that the surface where you have placed your twig vase may develop mold. Move the twig vases around until the twigs have dried, and you should not have any mold problems.

When all the twigs have dried, you can "refresh" the vase by substituting some of the dry twigs with fresh ones.

If you need to change out the glass tubes, replace one at a time. The twigs will fall apart if you take out all the test tubes at once.

# Elegant Flower Curtain

## Materials

* hollow stalks (*Persicaria*) or lichen-covered twigs
* spool wire
* stem wire
* drill
* test tubes
* flowers
* spray bottle

*A flower curtain made from hollow plant stalks (in this case, Persicaria, also known as knotweed or pinkweed) is easy to make and quite unique. The joints in these hollow stalks make waterproof casings that can be used as flower vases. All you have to do is drill a little hole and fill the hollow stalk with water. You may also use lichen-covered twigs for the construction of your flower curtain (see photograph on page 119). Such a construction is almost a complete decoration all by itself, without flowers or greenery! Still, you can decorate it with fresh flowers that you have found in forests or meadows, as well as cultivated flowers.*

You can make the curtain rather small or very large — explore the possibilities! There are many different types of *Persicaria*. Some are wild, while others are grown in parks and gardens. The type I have chosen to use can grow to about 10 feet, and the stalks look a little like bamboo.

## Instructions

* Cut the stalk into four pieces. Make sure that most of the pieces have joints. Tie the pieces together with spool wire, as described on page 14. You are making a frame. To stiffen the frame, tie stalks on the diagonal.

* Now you can drill holes into the hollow part of the stalk that has joints. Don't drill too far down, because the space you can fill with water becomes too small. You may want to drill two holes close by each other, so that you can insert several flower stalks into the same hollow space.

(opposite page)
*I have decorated a flower curtain made from knotweed stalks with phalaenopsis orchids and common bugloss.*

116

* Fill the hollow spaces with water, using a spray bottle. Then place the flower stalks as far down as possible toward the bottom of the hollow space. If you have chosen flowers that have long and flexible stems, you can shape the stems into graceful arches by attaching the flower head to the frame, using stem wire.

* Remember to add water to the hollow spaces as needed. You could drill a separate hole for the water so that you do not have to pull the flowers out every time you need to refill the hollow space.

* The green stalks will, after a while, become brown and shrink. If you still want to use the flower curtain, you must remember to re-tighten the spool-wire joints as the stalks dry.

## Instructions for a Flower Curtain Using Lichen-Covered Twigs:

* Make a frame of woven twigs by tying them together with spool wire, as described on page 14. Tie many twigs on the diagonal in all directions to stiffen the frame.

* Attach test tubes to the twigs, using spool wire or stem wire (depending upon the size of the tube). Attach each test tube at two points, one being at the top of the glass at the rim. The second point of attachment is your choice. You can cover the test tubes, completely or partially, by using lichen wrapped with stem wire. If you choose to leave the glass test tubes uncovered, that will also work very well. If you use plastic test tubes, you should always cover them with lichen.

* You can now place one or several flowers into each test tube, which, of course, have already been filled with water. Heavy flowers or those with long stems can be woven in between the twigs to get proper support, or you may choose to tie the flowers to the twigs with stem wire.

*(opposite page)*
*A flower curtain made with lichen-covered twigs and decorated with thistles and globeflowers.*

118

## Materials

* small, "aged" branches
* spool wire
* glass jar
* flowers

# Woven Twig Vase

*A mat woven with twigs can transform any ordinary container into a beautiful vase that will look stunning in even the most elegant interiors. Porcelain and crystal vases are not your only choices! The contrast between the polished, refined surfaces in your home and the rough, untreated twigs is intriguing and unexpected. If you weave a mat from freshly picked twigs, the weaving will loosen as the twigs dry. You cannot retighten the wires, so you must use very well-seasoned, "aged" twigs.*

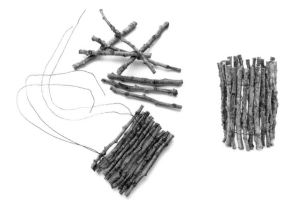

## Instructions

* Cut the branches into sticks of approximately the same length. Do not use bent sticks. Rough, straight sticks are charming and work well. You may also want to use colored branches, like green or red dogwood. Do not mix different types of sticks when making your mat. If your sticks are thin, you can use several in each "fold."

120

*For variety, place 2–3 twig vases of different heights close to each other. If you want to, you can push the flower stems in between the twigs and then into the water container. Clover and bird's-foot trefoil look good when used like this. In this picture, dwarf-birch branches have first been placed in the water to help keep the bird's-foot trefoil stems where you want them.*

* When you have your sticks ready, it is time to weave the sticks together in a long "row," using two long spool wires. Wrap the wires toward the ends of the sticks. Bend each wire and place a stick in the fold. Lock the stick into place by twisting the wire "legs" tightly around each other. Place another stick next to the previous one and twist the wires again. Continue the process until the mat is so long that you can wrap it around your glass jar (see photograph on page 120, center of the page). Finish by making a cylinder from the mat and attaching the wire "legs" to the first stick.

## Tip

You can make the twig mat much taller than the glass jar you are using. The twig vase will then help support flowers with long stems.

Beautiful, bashful liverleafs are resting on a hawthorn pillow.

## Materials

* hawthorn twigs
* floral wire
* spool wire
* stem wire
* assorted flowers and berries

(opposite page)
This hawthorn pillow features colorful, luscious ranunculus. The different-sized buds are an important part of the ornamental expression.

# Hawthorn "Pillow" with Flowers

When flowers rest on a background made from hawthorn twigs, their beauty is greatly enhanced. You may not even notice the simple wildflowers growing in the meadows, but you certainly will when they are placed on such a background. When you are ready to display your hawthorn pillow, place it over a dish with water, and make sure that the flowers you use to decorate the pillow are placed with their stems in this water. The flower heads should be resting on the pillow and should not extend beyond it.

Old hawthorn trees have charming, gnarled branches that often are covered with different-colored lichen. If you are lucky enough to discover a fallen hawthorn tree, be sure to collect as much material as possible for future use. If you come across other plants with unique characteristics, gather those also. You never know what will come in handy.

## Instructions

* Shape two equally large circles made from heavier metal floral wire (see "Wire Bouquet Holders" on page 40 to learn how to construct a metal-wire circle). The circle for this project has a diameter of 11¾ inches.

* Choose one of the circles and weave a web of metal wires by fastening an interior circle (4 inches in diameter) to the outer circle. Use metal floral wire for the inner circle. Use spool wire (smaller gauge) to create the web between the two circles. The web will resemble "slices of cake." The spaces between the wires can be quite open, because the small hawthorn twigs will start to create a denser web as you attach more and more twigs.

**1.**

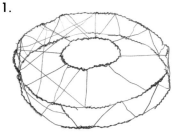

**2.**

*(opposite page)*
*Bashful, delicate flowers,*
*such as forget-me-nots,*
*liverleafs, wood anemones,*
*bird's-foot trefoil, and*
*bog star, look amazing on*
*a hawthorn pillow. Even*
*coarser plants like rose hips*
*or berries work very well as*
*decorations.*

* Attach the two large circles to each other, one "above" the other, leaving a gap of approximately 2 inches. Use a heavier metal floral wire and wrap it a couple of times around the top circle, and then a couple of times around the lower circle, alternatively. You will create a zigzag pattern (see photograph 1, on the left). Continue doing this until you have a zigzag pattern all around the circumference of the circles. Add additional support (and areas for flower placement) by wrapping stem wire at diagonal angles from the top to the bottom.

* Now you can begin to attach hawthorn twigs to the frame. Cover as much as possible of the frame's metal wires (see photograph 2, on the left). Attach each twig at two points, using stem wire. You can attach your twigs either to the frame or to other hawthorn twigs. Lock the twigs in place with 4–5 twists. Cut off the wire ends at once. It is best to finish the top surface before you start working on the side surface.

*Tip*

Do not despair if your metal frame is imperfect. You can straighten an imbalanced or crooked frame when you attach the hawthorn twigs.

# Lichen-Covered Twig Basket

*You can find paper lichen everywhere in forests — just look a little closer. Paper lichen is so much more than a growth on sad, dead spruce branches. When it is dry, it has a beautiful gray-green color, and the color becomes more turquoise in damp weather. Just gather branches together in a self-composed shape, and make your own "jewel" that you can decorate with flowers, or leave unadorned.*

It is best to use newly picked, soft branches. Moisten the lichen before use and spray the basket once in a while to refresh the lichen color.

## Instructions

* Make a circle from two heavier metal floral wires by connecting them as described on page 40. Attach six wires of equal length so that you end up with two "legs" of equal length at each point of attachment. Attach another wire to each "leg" to make it longer.

* Start making the basket by twisting each "leg" a few times around the neighboring "leg." Repeat the process while moving upwards, this time using the "twin leg" (the other "leg" in the pair) and attaching it to its "neighbor." Continue weaving until your wire basket is the desired size. You can continue to lengthen the "legs" by attaching additional wire lengths, if you want to make the basket larger. When you are done weaving, you will have a web of large or small holes, depending upon how closely you twisted the wires. If you think that the holes in your web are

## Materials

* lichen-covered twigs
* heavy metal flower wire
* stem wire
* test tubes

*(opposite page)*
*This lichen basket has been decorated with springtime blooms from the Norway maple (Acer plantanoides). The spring-green color is an exciting contrast to the gray-turquoise paper-lichen color. The decoration is enlivened by lit tea lights. They have been carefully placed in glass holders at a safe distance from any dry branches. There are many other suitable substitutes for the acer-tree flowers. Many wildflowers gathered in short bouquets would look very nice against the gray-turquoise lichen. Wood anemones would look beautiful, as would liverleafs, violets, bluebells, bloody cranesbills (Geranium sanguineum), bird's-foot trefoil, and forget-me-nots, all easily found in North America.*

too large, add additional wires across the openings as needed to make the holes smaller. Add wires to the bottom, crisscrossing the existing openings. The frame does not have to be perfect. You will cover most of the wires with branches. The most important thing is to make a rough "skeleton" in the shape you want.

* Start weaving lichen branches through the web. Use stem wire to attach them if they are hard to keep in place without ties. Do not attach the branches too closely. It is perfectly fine if the metal wires show. You want the basket to seem transparent. You can also make elegant arches by using long branches.

* Using stem wire, attach small test tubes to the inside of the basket. Place your flowers into the water-filled test tubes.

# Forest-Floor-Inspired Decorations

Learn to be observant when you go walking in the forest or through meadows. The natural landscape is filled with the most beautiful elements that invite you to employ them in all kinds of decorations. Strange roots, shimmering or lichen-covered stones, conifer twigs with cones — anything you may want is readily available.

## Instructions

* Saturate the floral foam with water and cover it with moss.

* Stick greenery — juniper, spruce, or pine branches, branches with leaves, or, preferably, berry-bush branches — into the moist floral foam. When you are done with the greenery, add flowers.

* Create a beautiful and surprising composition, using roots, stones, corky fungi, conifer cones, or, perhaps, edible mushrooms. Maybe you have collected items from your trips to the beach. There are endless possibilities. Be creative!

## Tip

If you are going to use wildflowers in a decoration, you should place those flowers which are tall in a natural setting above the other flowers in the decoration.

## Materials

* flat floral foam, placed in a waterproof container
* flowers
* greenery
* moss, and whatever else you may have found in nature

(opposite page)
This winter decoration is inspired by the natural forest landscape and has been placed on a mat woven from twigs. I started by placing a beautiful lichen-covered rock, a unique root, some spruce cones, and a lichen-covered twig in an interesting arrangement. Spruce branches, juniper branches, and berry-bush branches were added to create the green element. Anemones, tulips, and amaryllises have provided, refreshingly, the color element. The amaryllises have been placed in plastic test tubes, which have been pinned (see "Pinning" on page 15) so that they are securely fastened.

# A Birch-Bark Decoration for a Vase

*Simple and beautiful: one long and one short branch of an apple tree in bloom.*

There are many vases you can decorate with birch bark. The bark can emphasize the shape of the vase and make it sculptural. By decorating the vase in this way, you can use fewer flowers without the decoration seeming sparse. Birch bark from fallen trees is ideal. It often has a green sheen and beautiful patterns.

## Instructions

* Shape dried birch bark in such a manner that it harmonizes with the chosen vase. You may want to tear the bark to create some cracks, or trim it a little.

* Balance the birch bark over the vase's opening and place one or several flowers or branches into the vase.

## Materials

* a unique piece of birch bark
* a textured, opaque vase
* flowers

*(opposite page)*
*The picture shows sculptural birch bark on top of a black ceramic vase, decorated with five lupines and one lupine leaf.*

# Pattern for Birch-Bark Bouquet Holder

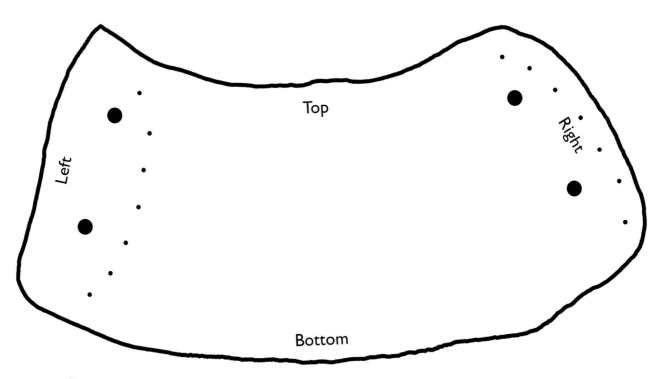

Left

Top

Right

Bottom

## Instruction

* When photocoping, enlarge the image by 60%.

# Index

Pages in *italics* indicate photos. Pages in **bold** indicate instructions for projects.